Smith
Street
Books

Vivienne Westwood

A to Z

INTRODUCTION

Vivienne Westwood was always something of a contradiction: the working-class girl who grew up to make couture, the school teacher who invented punk, the fashion designer who urged her fans to stop buying clothes. Her influence extends not just to fashion but to culture writ large. From the rebel yell of punk in the 1970s to the gender-blurring provocations of the New Romantics in the 1980s, to the introduction of sportswear and street culture on the runway – she was part of it all. Over the course of her nearly 60 years in fashion, she made clothes that were sexy and subversive, romantic and challenging – from graphic T-shirts that shocked with their provocative slogans, to corsets that shaped the body into an ultra-feminine form, to sky-high platform shoes that transformed their wearer's gait. She paid little attention to trends or marketability. Instead, she was driven by boundless curiosity – about the world, about history, about art, about the environment. Her lack of formal training as a dressmaker meant that she could see things others couldn't. The fashion press mocked or dismissed her, even as other designers copied her work. Her style was all her own.

Born Vivienne Isabel Swire in Glossop, Derbyshire, in 1941, she grew up in a British working-class family. It was an era in which women of her background were expected to become secretaries or librarians before settling down to motherhood. Vivienne very nearly followed the script: she trained as a primary school teacher, married young, and had a baby. But her exposure to life in London and her brief stint at art school offered a glimpse at another world. After her early marriage collapsed, Vivienne took her first steps to a life less ordinary. When the worldly, firebrand art student Malcolm McLaren turned up on the scene, Vivienne was smitten. They began a relationship and stoked the flames of each other's curiosity. They were young and dissatisfied with the conformity and provincialism they saw around them. Together, they wanted to change the world.

Unmoved by the hippie movement, they looked to the 1950s for inspiration, opening a boutique on King's Road called Let it Rock!, which traded in rock 'n' roll memorabilia and vintage clothing that Westwood would deftly repair and refashion. They were restless and innovative, repeatedly changing the name and ethos of the store to reflect their evolving interests: the shop transformed from selling '50s nostalgia to biker gear and DIY T-shirts (renamed Too Fast to Live, Too Young to Die), then turned to fetishwear and bondage aesthetics (SEX), to provocative punk styling (Seditionaries), and finally to the history-inspired romance of outcasts and pirates (Worlds End).

Malcolm and Vivienne's romantic relationship and professional collaboration ended soon after, but Vivienne's career was just beginning. Over the next decades, side by side with her husband and design partner Andreas Kronthaler, she would shape and reshape fashion, setting the agenda where others merely followed. Always an agitator, she used her fame as a designer to draw attention to the things she cared about – climate change, human rights, the ethical treatment of animals, liberty – and as time went on, her activism became her primary focus. 'I've constantly tried to provoke people into thinking afresh and for themselves, to escape their inhibitions and programming,' she once said. As both a designer and an activist, there was nothing she wanted more than to fight against convention – her enduring legacy is to inspire others to do the same.

NADIA BAILEY

is also for

Anarchy

Anarchy was punk's driving force, the rebel yell that galvanised the youth and sent the establishment into a moral panic. One of the most significant garments Vivienne made was the Anarchy shirt, which featured a portrait of Karl Marx, black handprints, and the phrase 'We are not afraid of ruins' – a slogan of the Italian fascist movement. 'We weren't only rejecting the values of the older generation, we were rejecting their taboos as well,' she explained.

...

Always on Camera

Looking to film star Marlene Dietrich as her muse, Vivienne's A/W 1992-93 collection was an ode to old Hollywood glamour, filtered through a Westwood lens. Models vamped and posed in double-breasted tweed trouser suits, chic headscarves, faux-fur coats, red-carpet-worthy gowns, a new version of Vivienne's Stature of Liberty corset, and distressed and printed mohair sweaters that recalled her provocative Seditionaries range.

...

Julian Assange

As a human rights activist, Vivienne threw her support behind people like Leonard Peltier, jailed for crimes he didn't commit; whistle-blower Chelsea Manning; and WikiLeaks founder Julian Assange, whose plight she once called the most important human rights case in history. 'Vivienne is effective because she can see through dogma,' said Julian. 'She is inconvenient; people cannot handle the consistency and seriousness with which she sticks to her politics [...] if we didn't have bloody-minded people just like Vivienne, we'd have no chance of changing our world for the better.'

For the *Anglomania* collection, Vivienne worked with heritage weavers Lochcarron of Scotland to design her own tartan – the MacAndreas, named after her husband and design partner Andreas Kronthaler. This fabric was added to the Scottish Register of Tartans that same year, and the Lochcarron of Scotland officially recognised the clan – a process that normally takes 200 years!

The *Anglomania* collection embodied Vivienne's belief in the exchange of ideas between France and England as the ideal union in fashion: 'On the English side we have tailoring and an easy charm, on the French side that solidity of design and proportion that comes from never being satisfied because something can always be done to make it better, more refined.'

Top supermodels of the 1990s, like Linda Evangelista, Christy Turlington and Kate Moss, walked in the show.

Naomi Campbell, wearing a royal blue velvet jacket, tartan kilt and cream rubber stockings, took a tumble from her 8½-inch platforms and fell straight into history – the photo of her sitting ruefully on the catwalk made headlines around the world. The shoes, instantly iconic, were subsequently acquired by the Victoria & Albert Museum in London.

A
is for
ANGLOMANIA

For her Autumn/Winter 1993–94 collection, *Anglomania*, shown in Paris, Vivienne Westwood looked back to 1780s France, when the fashionable French developed a passion for all things English. This outsider gaze on English culture – from its tailoring to the spontaneity of country charm to an appreciation of pastoral landscapes – imbued it with new life. It was this energy that Vivienne brought to the collection, coupled with her enduring fascination with English and Scottish traditions, realised through stout tweeds, double-breasted suits, woollen capes, tartan mini-kilt ensembles, corseted evening dresses and her Ghillie heels elevated to soaring heights with a vertiginous heel and platform. Models in pin curls showed off nightgowns and lingerie, faux-fur coats and neat bustle-back suits. A far cry from her punk days, the collection was an ode to 'distinction and elegance of dress', according to *The New York Times* – with a signature Westwood undercurrent of humour.

B

is for

BRITAIN

Vivienne Westwood was as British as they come – and her fashion career was built on referencing, mythologising and subverting British clothing and culture. In the early days, she and Malcolm McLaren were determined to transgress and destroy icons of British culture – they defaced the Union Jack and the Queen's portrait, and revelled in the shock it caused. In 1981, their first runway show drew inspiration from pirates as romantic, anti-imperialist outsiders – serving as a critique of the British Empire's role as a colonial plunderer. But Vivienne's relationship to Britain was multifaceted. While she frequently railed against British conservatism and classism, she was fascinated by British history, mythology, tradition and taboos, and wove complex references into her collections.

A fascination with English royalty runs through many of Vivienne's collections.

Both the *Mini-Crini* (Spring/Summer 1986) and *Harris Tweed* (A/W 1987–88) collections were partly inspired by the childhood wardrobes of the princesses Elizabeth and Margaret. Vivienne said at the time that she was inspired by the Queen and 'all the pomp and circumstance and Norman Hartnell you associate with her.'

Although the British fashion media failed to take her work seriously for many years – and the tabloid press never stopped poking fun at her eccentricities – Vivienne eventually achieved the honours she deserved: she was named Fashion Designer of the Year in both 1990 and 1991 by the British Fashion Council, and a year later received an OBE from the Queen at Buckingham Palace.

In 2006, she advanced from OBE to Dame Commander in recognition of her services to British fashion.

Since her earliest collections, Vivienne was passionate in her support of traditional fabrics and traditional British industries. She adored the fine tailoring of Savile Row and the craftsmanship in Scottish and English tweeds, and often commissioned heritage producers like John Smedley and Lochcarron of Scotland to create custom fabrics for her ranges.

Vivienne was dissatisfied with modern Britain. In the late 1980s and early '90s – known as her Pagan Years – she advocated for a return to classicism and the freedoms of the ancient world. 'My theme for the last year or two has been that Britain must go pagan,' she said. 'We have no culture, we're in the age of the philistine. I believe that culture's the lifeblood of civilisation and I don't believe we're civilised at all.'

B

is also for

Books

As a former school teacher, it's perhaps no surprise that Vivienne was a staunch advocate for reading. Early in her career, when she was struggling financially, books on history and anthropology served as her primary source of inspiration – she was able to travel to different places and different eras without leaving her flat. She believed that books opened the mind to other people's lives and experiences: 'You only live once if you don't read,' she once said. 'If you read books, you can live a hundred lives.'

...

Buy Less

When it came to addressing overconsumption in the fashion industry, Vivienne had a simple solution: *Buy Less, Choose Well, Make it Last*. She advocated against sweatshop-produced, trend-driven fast fashion that falls apart after a couple of wears and recommended people invest in high-quality garments. She told *The Guardian*, 'We need to get back to having fewer things, and treasuring what we have. That's why I defend high fashion.'

...

François Boucher

Vivienne discovered the work of François Boucher in the Wallace Collection in London. His bucolic paintings of bosomy shepherdesses, cherubs and fluffy lambs appealed to her love of the classical and sensuous. 'There is a link between art and fashion,' she said. 'I couldn't design a thing if I didn't look at art.' She went on to use photographic prints of paintings, such as *Daphnis and Chloe* and *Hercules and Omphale*, throughout her collections.

C

is also for

Café Society

Café Society (S/S 1994) was inspired by the gatherings of artists and philosophers around the cafés of late-19th-century Paris. Partly an homage to the couturier Charles Worth, the collection featured structured skirt suits and slim, elegant silhouettes, contrasted with corsets, knickers and sky-high platforms. 'The models looked incredible because they had all this hair and lots of white make-up, and incredibly high shoes,' Vivienne said. 'I remember saying I didn't know whether they were monsters or goddesses, knowing that that's a statement that the press kind of like. But you really thought, they are freaks, definitely. They look so freaky, so different, but so beautiful.'

...

Joseph Corré

Born to Vivienne Westwood and Malcolm McClaren, Joseph Corré was drafted into the family business at an early age, becoming involved in the business side of the Westwood label at 19, and occasionally modelling in shows. He went on to co-found the lingerie label Agent Provocateur, but is perhaps best known for destroying an estimated £6-million-worth of his punk rock memorabilia in protest of the commodification of punk, as well as to draw attention to the climate crisis. 'Everyone's obsessed with the price of destroying this stuff, but you have to think about value – what is really important,' he said. 'Why is that stuff of any value whatsoever? Because it represented a moment in time when people thought they could do something. And then it just turned into a pose. And it's been a pose ever since.'

For *Vive la Cocotte* in 1995–96, she imagined a corset inspired by nudity itself, in which the 'naked' torso was an artfully constructed and embroidered bodice complete with rhinestone nipples – made by the famous corsetier, Mr Pearl.

'For me the focus of a woman is the waist,' said Vivienne of why she resurrected the corset for a new generation. 'And this corset we made: it is really, really sexy. Low-cut. It held the waist in. It forced the breasts up. That was the whole point, that it was pushing – that's what those corsets did, they pushed the breasts up. And people just loved it.'

Vivienne first experimented with corsetry back when she created fetishwear collections at SEX in the 1970s, then turned the corset into outerwear in her couture collections of the late 1980s, including *Harris Tweed* (A/W 1987–88) and *Time Machine* (A/W 1988–89).

For the S/S 1997 collection *Vive la Bagatelle*, Vivienne showed a corseted wedding dress on a model who walked the runway with her hands bound behind her back and her eyes covered by a blindfold – a witty embodiment of the saying 'love is blind.'

The Bagatelle corset featured a romantic neckline anchored to an 18th-century-inspired flat corset, and went on to become one of the staples of the Vivienne Westwood bridal range.

C is for CORSETS

History, and historical dress, was a constant source of inspiration for Vivienne Westwood's designs – and she was among the first contemporary designers to look to the corset for inspiration. The garment was introduced to European courts in the 15th century and was worn by women (and sometimes men) up until the 20th century. Known for moulding a woman's figure into whatever shape was deemed most desirable at the time, the corset has associations with sexuality, power, oppression and control. In the 1980s, Vivienne was inspired after seeing a 19th-century corset that her friend and mentor, the art historian Gary Ness, had acquired at a flea market to consider how the corset might be transformed into outerwear. She then borrowed an 18th-century copy from a theatrical costumier, which she used as a template to create her own version, modernising key elements to make it more wearable. Vivienne's version used stretch panels on the side and a zip fastening instead of lacing – but kept the iconic shape that put so much emphasis on a woman's cleavage. The corset quickly became a Westwood signature.

D is for DRESSING UP

The theme was the last days of the British Empire. *Dressing Up* (A/W 1991–92) marked Vivienne Westwood's return to showing at Paris Fashion Week after a hiatus of six years – a move made possible by the designer Azzedine Alaïa, who let her use his showroom free of charge. The collection embraced eclecticism, overt maximalism and extended hemlines, in a season when most other designers were championing pared-back minimalism, deconstruction and sportswear. The collection included tailored 'love jackets' with large lapels that formed a heart when fastened up, leopard-print coats and hats, slinky tube dresses that could be worn short or pulled down to a demure length, and courtly 'DL' jackets, which were named in honour of the film *Dangerous Liaisons* (1988), and based on an 18th-century frock coat. Jeans were printed with cherubs or photographs of the interiors of an 18th-century chateau, and rubber mackintoshes were emblazoned with cherubs from a Fragonard painting. For Vivienne, the collection served as a rallying cry, advocating for a return to glamour, elegance and the joy of dressing up.

The *Dressing Up* collection received mixed reviews from the British and US press, but in France it was a hailed as a success. Top designers like Jean-Paul Gaultier and Christian Lacroix attended. After the show, Yves Saint Laurent, Karl Lagerfeld and others sent Vivienne congratulatory bouquets.

'Fashion is always about reacting against what has become orthodox,' Vivienne once said. 'And as sex is the strongest influence in fashion, to play around with new sexual motifs is to be in the avant-garde.' To this end, *Dressing Up* prominently featured codpieces for women, which were attached suggestively to the front of skirts and knickers, or used as decorative elements on jackets and corsets.

The mood of this collection was pure, old-fashioned opulence. 'Imagine it's 1900,' said Vivienne. 'You're living in a castle and rummaging through Grandfather's chest with all his bits and bobs from the Empire.'

is also for

Dressed to Scale

Vivienne Westwood's A/W 1998–99 collection, *Dressed to Scale*, was a surrealist jaunt through a variety of Westwood signatures made fresh through distortion and exaggeration. Here, cuts were designed to reshape the body, with lapels stretched to shoulder width, nipped waists gave the illusion of fuller hips, and buttons were blown up to enormous size. Models wore heavily powdered faces and cupid's bow lips, giving them a caricature-like look that heightened the Surrealist feel of the collection. It was an ode to the beauty of the constructed: 'The whole point about civilisation is to be as artificial as possible,' Vivienne pronounced.

...

Down to No. 10

In 2021, Andreas Kronthaler for Vivienne Westwood presented a collection called *Down to No. 10* under extraordinary circumstances. Designed and presented under COVID-19 restrictions, it was delivered virtually via images and a series of short films featuring Vivienne and Andreas, along with models Sara Stockbridge and Vita Leandra. Featuring iconic Westwood cuts rendered in sustainable fabrics, the collection marked the 40th anniversary of Vivienne Westwood's catwalk debut, her 50th year in fashion, Andreas' 30th year of working with Vivienne and the 10th collection of Andreas Kronthaler for Vivienne Westwood.

E

is also for

Eccentricities

Vivienne's eccentricities were many: her singular look, her marriage to a man 25 years her junior, her disdain for popular culture, her tendency to go without underwear. She lived in the same cramped council flat in south London for 30 years, rode her bicycle everywhere, and often slept in her workshop. If people were perplexed by her designs or confused by the things she found attractive, she wasn't bothered by it: 'I think I'm the only one who is original,' she said. 'I don't see anyone doing anything that doesn't come from me.'

...

Education

As a child, Vivienne was sent to a church school – a conservative institution that emphasised a respect for the Church of England and the monarchy. But it was there that she first had proper sewing and embroidery lessons. Later, she went to Glossop Grammar, where she excelled at English Literature and History. When her family moved to London, it gave her the opportunity to enrol at Harrow Art School, where she studied jewellery-making and silversmithing for one term. It was to remain her only formal training in design.

...

England

'Englishness is vital to what I do,' Vivienne once declared. 'It's about cut, it's about irony and it's about risk-taking.' But her identification with England was tempered by a healthy dose of irreverence: 'I am English, and I parody the English, with the hope that my clothing will have an international significance.'

The 'Cul cage' wire bustle, which caused such a sensation, was created by Andreas Kronthaler's father, who used his skill as a blacksmith to forge them. It was based on the strapontin wire bustles of the late 1880s, adapted to be smaller, lighter, and easier to wear.

Vivienne credited her interest in the bustle pad and the hourglass silhouette to her husband, Andreas Kronthaler. 'It came out of a conversation with Andreas about my underwear and the way women's bottoms move,' she said.

'Art takes a conversation, sometimes a conversation between a man and a woman, about sex,' said Vivienne.

For this show, models wore spindly stiletto heels that made them sway as they walked. 'It's like a chain reaction,' Vivienne said. 'Once you have the high heels on, then with the big bottom, the tiny waist, everything starts to move … !'

A tribute to the power of female sexuality, *Erotic Zones* (S/S 1995) showcased Vivienne Westwood's skill in using unusual silhouettes to provoke, titillate and delight. Held in the stark show spaces beneath the Louvre in Paris, the collection featured dresses with nipped-in waists and padded hips, accented by an innovative wire bustle, and designed to endow the wearer with an hourglass figure. Elsewhere, there were tailored trouser suits, inspired by the portraits of German Expressionist painter Otto Dix, with fitted jackets and high-waisted trousers, wide corselets, saucy wide-brimmed hats and elegant fishtail evening gowns. 'Erotic zones are sometimes about concealment,' said Vivienne. 'It is playing around with proportion and the things that you expose on the body.' For Vivienne, it was all about the silhouette: she found the juxtaposition of a narrow waist with an exaggerated hip and bottom to be extremely exciting. In the show program, she made her intentions clear: 'The idealisation of woman can never be completed.'

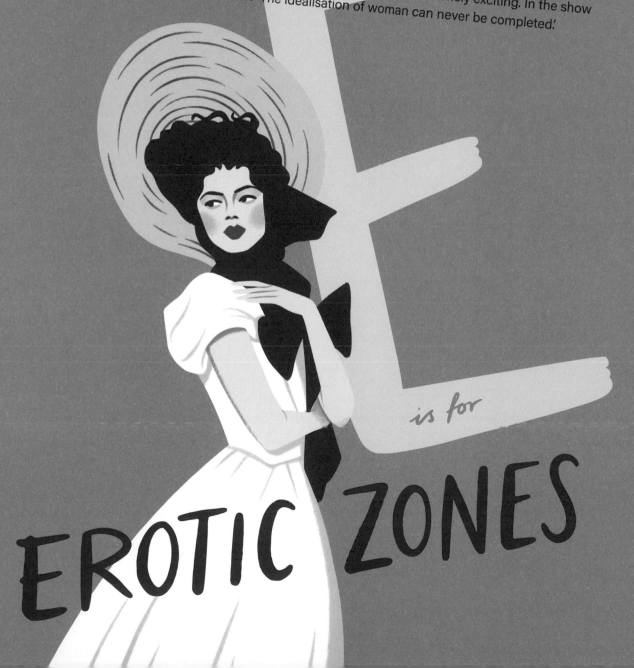

is for

EROTIC ZONES

FRAGRANCE

is for

Vivienne Westwood launched her first fragrance in 1998. Christened Boudoir, it was created by legendary perfumer Martin Gras of Dragoco to evoke a sense of privacy, intimacy and seduction – just like its namesake. 'A boudoir is a dressing room and a place to get undressed,' said Vivienne. 'It signifies a woman's space, a place where she is on intimate terms with herself, where she sees her faults and her potential.' The fragrance was envisioned as one that would make a man turn his head after a woman as her scent wafted past him – and one legend suggests that Vivienne requested something that recalled certain parts of the female anatomy! With fresh, floral, powdery top notes, an opulent rose-drenched heart spiked with ashy tobacco, and a base that purred with vanilla, spice and animalic notes, Boudoir was somehow both classic and modern – like an Elizabethan queen with a safety pin through her nose.

Two years after Boudoir, Vivienne launched a fragrance called Libertine – a luscious, sparkling scent inspired by history and the English monarchy. Libertine combined fruity top notes of grapefruit, pineapple and passionfruit, a floral heart of lily of the valley, honeysuckle, bergamot and rose, and a sensual base of oak moss, patchouli, musk and amber.

Libertine won many fans – including *Sex and the City's* Carrie Bradshaw. A bottle of the perfume can be seen on the windowsill of Carrie's apartment in the season six episode *Hop, Skip and a Week*.

After the success of Boudoir and Libertine, Vivienne went on to release a range of perfumes inspired by her history, legacy and fascinations, including the name of her boutique (Let it Rock!), and the name of a fashion era in her history (Anglomania).

The *Alice* collection, inspired by Lewis Carroll's *Alice in Wonderland*, includes the fragrances Naughty Alice, Cheeky Alice, Flirty Alice and Sunny Alice.

Feminism
'I am not a feminist,' Vivienne once declared, 'because I do find that feminism is too closely linked to a puritan attitude.' She found the feminist movement at odds with her ideals of pagan sensuality and love of provocative clothing that played up feminine sexuality. 'I can't see how anyone would object to a lady at the height of her beauty, without any clothes on whatsoever,' she said. But if she was at odds with the second-wave feminists, perhaps it was because she was ahead of her time. She stood for body-positivity, took a strong stance against ageism, encouraged gender fluidity and showed women that they could feel sexy and desirable in a way that didn't conform to society's narrow ideas of beauty. Although she didn't call herself a feminist, she never asked women to be anything but themselves.

...

Five Centuries Ago
One of Vivienne's most overtly historical collections, *Five Centuries Ago* (A/W 1997–98) was inspired by the court costumes of Elizabethan England. Dramatic silhouettes featured Tudor-style bodices, square necklines and enormous farthingale hooped skirts; models also wore rubber masks and leather corsets, harking back to her Seditionaries days. The press noted her growing impact across the fashion industry: 'It is difficult to find a single collection in Paris without some trace of her influence, be it punk or an earnest rendering of historic dress,' wrote a critic for *The New York Times*.

G

is also for

Gender

Throughout her career, Vivienne experimented with blurring the lines between masculine and feminine. In *Always on Camera* (A/W 1992–93), her old Hollywood starlets wore va-va-voom outfits paired with neat pencil moustaches, while several collections featured codpieces for women. For the *Unisex* collection of A/W 2015–16, Vivienne cast a male model to play the Westwood bride, who closed the show wearing a chest-baring bronze corset and matching ruffled skirt.

...

Gold Label

Vivienne Westwood's demi-couture line represented the purest form of her genius – her most considered, forward-thinking, provocative designs. In 2016, the line was renamed Andreas Kronthaler for Vivienne Westwood to reflect Andreas' role in the business. Today, the range continues its iconoclast spirit under his sole creative direction.

...

Get a Life

In 2010, Vivienne began keeping an online diary – a place where she could articulate her unique vision for the world and inspire others to fight for climate justice and human rights as passionately as she did. Her diaries serve as an unapologetic call to arms: 'I call the diaries *Get a Life* as that's how I feel: you've got to get involved, speak out and take action,' she explained. Spanning fashion, art and writing, human rights, climate change and activism, the diaries provided a fascinating insight into her psyche. Her words were later collected and published as a book of the same name.

The collection was a triumph – *Marie Claire* immediately pulled clothes for a cover shoot, while legendary photographer Steven Meisel photographed them for US *Vogue*.

The show paid tribute to the idea of a glamorous hotel lobby as a place to see and be seen.

'My clothes have a scent, a feeling of "I know it but I don't know what it is." They have a certain type of nostalgia, which – for me – is how I would define glamour,' said Vivienne of the 1950s feel of the collection. 'They are part of the story of human culture. Even though it's all references to the past, they are synthesised to a point where they couldn't have been done at any other time.'

CHECK IN

Those appearing in the show included men and women, old and young, professional models and amateurs, and even Vivienne herself, in her catwalk debut.

Taking its title from a 1932 film starring Greta Garbo, *Grand Hotel* (S/S 1993) marked the evolution of Vivienne's interest in the silhouettes and techniques of haute couture, inspired by the classic designs of Yves Saint Laurent and Christian Dior. In this collection, Vivienne presented a homage to 1950s tailoring with satin pyjama suits, demure, full-circle skirts, off-the-shoulder necklines and Riviera-inspired colours, as though the audience had been transported to the lobby of a mid-century South American hotel through which passed an exotic array of well-dressed people. The collection also featured denim adorned with 18th-century prints inspired by fabrics in the V&A collection, precariously high heels, and togas emblazoned with prints of endangered animal species. The message was one of environmental conservation – a cause that would become increasingly important to Vivienne as time went on.

is for

GRAND HOTEL

H

is for

HISTORY

'I get my ideas because I'm interested in the past,' said Vivienne Westwood. When it came to inspiration, there was nothing more exciting to her than history – whether that was historical dress, classical art, or the ideas of seminal philosophers. She had a voracious appetite for visiting museums and galleries, could drop quotes by great thinkers into casual conversation, and regularly reworked historical clothing for her own designs, from the corset, to the crinoline, to the codpiece. 'I take something from the past which has a sort of vitality that has never been exploited,' she said. 'You take something that already exists and you get so involved with it that, in the end, you do something original because you overlay your own ideas.' Perhaps more than any other designer, she had an innate sense of how historical clothing could be studied, dismantled, reconstructed, and reworked into something that was both modern and desirable.

'Knowledge of the past lends perspective to the present and insight into the future. All my ideas come from studying the ideas of the past. I design clothes in the hope of breaking convention.'

Her genius wasn't in mere replication of existing historical designs – it was the way she filtered past styles through a contemporary lens in a way that gave them new life. Speaking of her 1995–96 collection, *Vive la Cocotte*, she said, 'I was able finally to produce a silhouette that had never been done before, nor could it have been, because it was a synthesis put together in the present.'

Ultimately, Vivienne trusted her own design instincts – but history was a well she drew from again and again for inspiration. The clothes she made were grounded in the standards of excellence set by history's greatest couturiers.

'I'm not trying to do something different,' she reflected. 'I'm trying to do the same thing but in a different way.'

For Vivienne, the past was an essential part of her design practice.

is also for

Hypnos

Hypnos (S/S 1984) was a collection that appeared sporty and modern, but was inspired by Greek mythology and the first Olympics. It featured fluorescent pink and green garments made from synthetic sports fabric, jockstraps lifted from gay subcultures, matching track outfits complete with knee-pads, and rubber buttons shaped like phalluses. The range cannily predicted the impact that sportswear would later have on fashion and was selected to be shown in Tokyo at Hanae Mori's 'Best of Five' global fashion awards. It was also Vivienne's first collection that wasn't in collaboration with Malcolm McLaren.

...

Harris Tweed

An ode to Englishness that only Vivienne Westwood could create, *Harris Tweed* (A/W 1987–88) was both a celebration and subversion of British culture. Taking its name from the traditional Scottish woven fabric – and shamelessly appropriating the Harris Tweed Authority's royal orb logo – the collection featured models in neat A-line coats, schoolboy-inspired blazers and mini-crini skirts, with their lipstick smeared as though they were naughty debutantes who'd been kissing their boyfriends. Elsewhere, they frolicked in fabric crowns and faux ermine tippets, adding to the impression of playing dress-up as royalty. Vivienne mused, 'Here I've taken the vocabulary of royalty – the traditional British symbols, and used it to my own advantage. I've utilised the conventional to make something unorthodox.'

I

is also for

Italy

Italy was perhaps the first region where Vivienne Westwood found critical acclaim and an appreciative audience – long before her home country began to take her work seriously. From the early 1990s, Vivienne produced her clothing in Italy, a move that made commercial expansion possible. 'For years I struggled to manufacture in England, and the breakthrough came for me when I finally started to produce in Italy,' she said. Given Vivienne's unique aesthetic, there were sometimes some kinks to be ironed out: 'In Italy they take cheap cloth and make it look expensive, and I take expensive cloth and make it look cheap,' she once complained. 'They just don't understand what I'm trying to do!'

...

I Groaned With Pain

In 1973, Vivienne Westwood came up with a simple design for a T-shirt – two squares of fabric sewn together on the outside, with the edges left raw. 'It looked and felt sexy, subversive, full of style,' remembered Malcolm McLaren. Pre-empting the pornographic T-shirts they would later sell at SEX, Vivienne and Malcolm printed the shirt with the racy opening paragraph of an erotic novel called *Helen and Desire* (1954) by beat writer Alexander Trocchi, which began with the phrase 'I groaned with pain.' They saw no problem with copying the text wholesale: 'Plagiarism is what the world's about,' Malcolm once said. 'If you don't start seeing things and stealing because you were inspired by them, you'd be stupid.'

Books and classical art were common sources of inspiration for Vivienne, but occasionally her work referenced the contemporary – David Lynch's film *The Elephant Man* (1980) inspired the hats shown in the *Savage* collection (S/S 1982), while *Punkature* (S/S 1983) incorporated prints inspired by Ridley Scott's *Blade Runner* (1982).

Vivienne placed a huge amount of emphasis on the value of imagination – even if it meant other people copying her designs: 'If people can't afford my clothes, they can make their own. Let them chop their T-shirt in half and then use their imagination. I'm all for people doing their own thing.'

In 2011, Vivienne wrote a letter to Marc Jacobs drawing a link between imagination, design, and her commitment to bringing about positive change in the world: 'I am especially happy at the moment because I feel that everything is coming together – that I can use fashion as a medium to express my ideas to fight for a better world; and because of the credibility fashion gives me a voice, and this in turn helps the fashion and keeps me stimulated and inspired ... .'

I is for IMAGINATION

Vivienne Westwood originally studied to be a teacher and educated young children for five years before turning to fashion. But whether she was in a classroom or her design studio, she always sought to impart knowledge and share her curiosity about history, art, politics, culture and the world at large. She was passionate about seeking out knowledge as a way of forming a unique point of view: 'If you accept that something is right, just because everyone believes it, then you're not thinking. You have to look at other people's points of view and then make up your own mind.' Vivienne found inspiration from wildly eclectic sources – from a book on voodoo practices to the works of William Shakespeare – and all these references came together in her imagination to create something unprecedented and new. Equally, she understood that her own work could spark the imagination of others – which is why she placed so much emphasis on incorporating her beliefs into her runway shows and even into the designs themselves. 'I use fashion as a medium,' she told *Interview Magazine*. 'I put things in the show that send a message.'

J is for JEWELLERY

Just like her clothing, Vivienne Westwood's jewellery designs embodied a singular elegance – a combination of old-fashioned glamour and punk rock subversion. Her interest in jewellery went back to her teenage years – after completing her School Certificate at Glossop Grammar in Derbyshire, she applied to Harrow Art School in London and was accepted into a jewellery-making and silversmithing course. A single term of this course was her only formal training in design. In the 1960s, her first foray into design was making jewellery and selling it at the Portobello Road markets – later, when she and Malcolm McLaren opened their store on King's Road, they sold chains, safety pins and razor blades (ground down with a nail file) as jewellery for the burgeoning punk scene. Once Vivienne had struck out on her own as a designer, she made jewellery an integral part of her brand – she was particularly interested in using pearls, long associated with royalty and the upper class, in new and subversive ways. She first showed pearls in her *Harris Tweed* collection of 1987–88, where pearl necklaces were styled on both men and women. The three-row choker was first shown in the *Portrait* collection of 1990–91; since then, it has become one of the house's most iconic and sought-after designs.

Iconography such as bones, razor blades, safety pins and devil horns paid tribute to her rebellious roots.

'I thought the idea of one pearl earring or [...] three strands of pearls with a pearl drop in the middle was typical of all jewellery,' recalled Vivienne. 'You could fit it with practically any period and it would look all right. So I sort of chose things in that way, I wanted them to be complete, as archetypal as they could be.'

On the other end of the spectrum, Vivienne often styled her models – and herself – in jewellery that harkened back to her early days as the Queen of Punk.

'A man in a pearl necklace is much more interesting than a man in a skirt,' Vivienne once said.

Vivienne Westwood's Armour Ring found a cult following after it was featured heavily in *Nana*, a popular Japanese manga series that later became an anime. In it, the character Nana Osaki wears outfits inspired by early Harajuku subcultures, mixed with Vivienne Westwood designs. Her signature is the Armour Ring, which she wears in almost every chapter of the manga publications and episode of the series.

J is also for

Japan

One of the ironies of Vivienne Westwood's life was that for much of her career she was much more famous in places like France and Italy than she was in the UK. But nowhere appreciated her more than Japan, where her references to British heritage, classical French art, punk ethos, and exacting attention to craft resonated with the fashion-hungry youth. In return, Vivienne appreciated her Japanese fans because they took her designs seriously – people didn't point and laugh at her like they did when she took to the streets in Britain wearing her mini-crini and rocking horse shoes. Her influence in Japan stretches back to the *Nostalgia of Mud* collection (A/W 1982–83), which was creatively in sync with the body-obscuring fashions that Rei Kawakubo and Yohji Yamamoto were doing at the time. By the early 1980s, her clothing was stocked in Harajuku boutiques, with her *Seditionaries* range proving immediately popular. For a long time, Japanese fans of the brand would have to make a pilgrimage to London to get their hands on the latest designs, but in 1996, a flagship boutique opened in Tokyo – the brand's first outside of the UK. Throughout the '90s and into the new millennium, Westwood clothing was a favourite among the fashionably dressed youth and helped define the Harajuku look popularised in the influential *FRUiTS* magazine. To this day, Japan remains one of the biggest markets for Vivienne Westwood clothing.

is also for

Kink

Born from a desire to challenge British sensibilities, Vivienne Westwood often incorporated elements of fetish and kink into her designs. This was most obvious during the SEX era, when she and Malcolm McLaren offered 'rubberwear for the office' and later with Seditionaries, when they began to 'crossbreed the biker look with fetish-wear,' creating bondage-influenced clothing splashed with pornographic imagery. For Vivienne, the graphic T-shirts were an easy way to push people's buttons: 'With them you could find out where people's sore spots are and how free you really are,' she said. 'Sex is the thing that bugs English people more than anything else, so that's where I attack.'

...

Kilts

Long before she started designing them, Vivienne Westwood wore kilts. Malcolm McLaren recalled her wearing homemade knits and kilts, paired with wispy hair and fur coats ('I was into the dolly bird look,' said Vivienne). Later, when Vivienne was designing the *Seditionaries* range, she reworked the kilt into a provocatively short version, which was paired with bondage-inspired gear. As her aesthetic developed and she turned to historical dress as her primary source of inspiration, the kilt remained a touchstone, appearing in numerous collections as well as in her own wardrobe, which she wore with rocking horse shoes, white socks and a twinset. 'They feel wonderful – you feel so heroic wearing a kilt.'

'In one second, in just a second, a split second, everything slowed down,' said Andreas of the moment he first saw Vivienne. 'I thought she was – she is – so chic. Maybe more than anything, that was my first impression.'

To Vivienne

In 2016, Vivienne Westwood announced that the name of her mainline collection would be changed to Andreas Kronthaler for Vivienne Westwood.

In a love letter to Vivienne, written in 2018, Andreas paid homage to Vivienne as his collaborator, partner, teacher, muse and 'the best-dressed woman in any room.'

Formerly known as Vivienne Westwood Gold Label, the change reflected an acknowledgement of how integral Andreas was to the brand.

is for

ANDREAS KRONTHALER

Andreas Kronthaler: husband, design partner, muse. The story begins in Vienna, where Vivienne Westwood had taken up a position as a visiting professor of fashion at the Vienna Academy of Arts. There she met Andreas Kronthaler, a 23-year-old design student who impressed her with his talent and intelligence. Soon, she offered him work in her studio and within months they were living together. The couple married secretly in May 1992, when Vivienne was 50 and Andreas was 25 – a fact that the tabloids made much of when they broke the story. But their partnership proved to be lifelong, both creatively and romantically. Andreas became an integral part of Vivienne's brand, and the two took on a collaborative design process, motivating and inspiring one another – Vivienne, for example, credited Andreas with introducing her to the potential of couture, which led to the creation of the *Grand Hotel* collection. 'When two people have different talents but are equally strong it's difficult to say who does what,' said Vivienne. 'Usually the work is a co-operation and the two of us reach a level that I could not reach alone.'

is for

LET IT ROCK

In 1971, when London's cool kids were dressing as hippies and flower children, Vivienne Westwood and Malcolm McLaren opened a stall selling old records and rock 'n' roll ephemera from the 1950s. The stall was located inside a store called Paradise Garage, which sold vintage denim, imported from the US, as well as deadstock Hawaiian shirts, baseball jackets, boiler suits, dungarees and more. But Paradise Garage was short-lived and soon Vivienne and Malcolm expanded to take over the whole space at 403 King's Road, redecorating it to look like a mid-century living room and filling it with James Dean memorabilia, photos ripped from risqué magazines, rock 'n' roll fanzines and original 1950s clothing, which they sourced from junk shops and markets in the unfashionable suburbs. Rock 'n' roll songs by the likes of Elvis Presley, Little Richard, Chuck Berry and more blasted from a jukebox; outside, bright pink letters announced the shop's name and ethos: 'Teddy Boys are Forever – Rock is our business.' When the store sold out of the original Teddy Boy clothing that Vivienne had sourced, Malcolm asked her to start making copies – setting her on a path that would change her life.

Thanks to stores like Let it Rock!, King's Road became a destination for the young, the cool and the fashion conscious, and attracted famous faces like Iggy Pop, the New York Dolls, David Bowie and Marianne Faithfull.

With the attention to detail of an archivist, Vivienne began to unpick, copy and duplicate vintage 1950s pieces, like drainpipe trousers and drape jackets, then remake them using authentic fabrics, buttons and linings from the same era.

Clothing sourced from Let it Rock! appeared in the film *That'll Be The Day*, starring Ringo Starr and David Essex.

London

Vivienne Westwood moved to London in 1958 – and it was this moment that she would later come to see as the most significant in her life. 'I was nearly seventeen, and everything in my world changed.' The transition to London life wasn't an easy one for Vivienne, who found the change of pace overwhelming and the people arrogant and unkind. 'In London you feel your back's to the wall from the very beginning,' she recalled. But London introduced her to fashion, art, music and culture, and gave her the stimulation she needed to diverge from the conventional path. Aside from a brief stint living in Italy, Vivienne was a Londoner for the rest of her life.

...

Les Femmes ne Connaissant Pas Toute Leur Coquetterie

Playing on her fascination with historical dress from the 18th and 19th centuries, *Les Femmes ne Connaissant Pas Toute Leur Coquetterie* (S/S 1996) presented Vivienne Westwood at her most commercially accessible. The collection featured simple chemises, toile de jouy prints, sharply androgynous suits and tight tailoring. With its title translating to 'Women don't know the full extent of their coquettishness' – a maxim by French writer and moralist François de La Rochefoucauld – the collection embodied Vivienne's love of dressing the female form. Nowhere was this clearer than in the collection's closing look, worn by supermodel Linda Evangelista: a sweeping, emerald-green gown that draped tantalisingly from one shoulder, inspired by the art of Antoine Watteau.

M
is also for

Manifestos

The manifesto was one of Vivienne Westwood's favourite forms of communication. Whether printed on a T-shirt, handed out at her shows, or published online, Vivienne used manifestos to instruct, confront and galvanise – from extolling the benefits of culture over consumption to educating people on the dangers of climate change.

...

Jordan Mooney

Born Pamela Rooke, Jordan Mooney was hired to work in the SEX boutique. Thanks to her fearless personal style, she soon became an attraction in her own right. Jordan's gravity-defying hair, aggressively punk make-up and flesh-baring outfits made her instantly recognisable on the streets of London. 'She eclipsed every other thing in sight,' recalled club owner Michael Costiff. 'Jordan was just like a goddess.' Her impact on punk was so great that she has sometimes been referred to as 'the first Sex Pistol.'

...

Mini-Crini

In the mid-1980s, the dominant trend in fashion saw women embracing a strong, masculinised look built on gym-toned bodies and power suits – but with *Mini-Crini* (S/S 1986), Vivienne Westwood proposed an entirely different aesthetic. Inspired by the ballet *Petrushka* and a photograph of the Queen as a child wearing a double-breasted princess coat, the collection featured girlish leotards, short skirts scaffolded by a lightweight crinoline, schoolgirl blazers, bloomers and naïve prints. The collection was hugely influential, with the mini-crini look quickly adopted by other designers across the world.

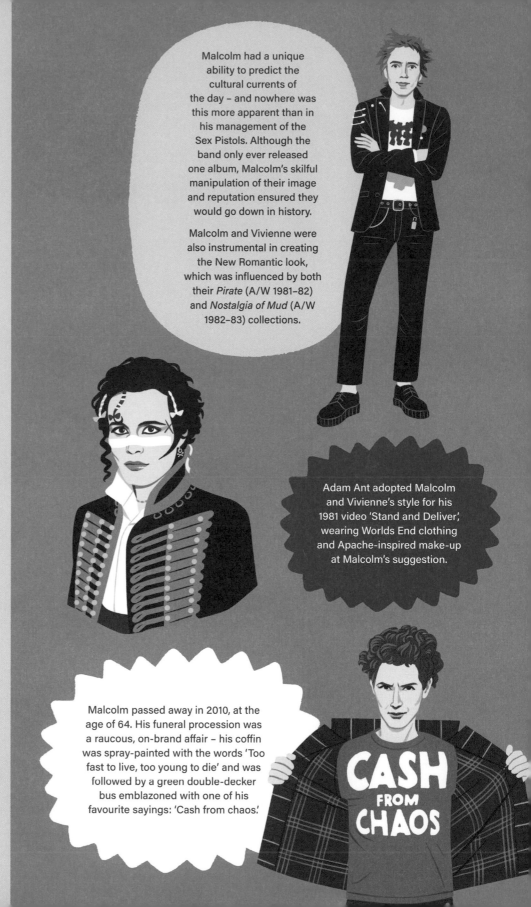

Malcolm had a unique ability to predict the cultural currents of the day – and nowhere was this more apparent than in his management of the Sex Pistols. Although the band only ever released one album, Malcolm's skilful manipulation of their image and reputation ensured they would go down in history.

Malcolm and Vivienne were also instrumental in creating the New Romantic look, which was influenced by both their *Pirate* (A/W 1981–82) and *Nostalgia of Mud* (A/W 1982–83) collections.

Adam Ant adopted Malcolm and Vivienne's style for his 1981 video 'Stand and Deliver,' wearing Worlds End clothing and Apache-inspired make-up at Malcolm's suggestion.

Malcolm passed away in 2010, at the age of 64. His funeral procession was a raucous, on-brand affair – his coffin was spray-painted with the words 'Too fast to live, too young to die' and was followed by a green double-decker bus emblazoned with one of his favourite sayings: 'Cash from chaos.'

M
is for

MALCOLM McLAREN

In 1965, Vivienne Westwood had split up with her first husband, Derek Westwood. She was working as a primary school teacher when she met a skinny, red-haired student named Malcolm McLaren. Malcolm was a troublemaker with big ideas and Vivienne was smitten. They began a relationship, quickly had a child, and moved in together in a flat in London (which Vivienne would call home for the next 30 years). Malcolm was voraciously interested in culture – in fashion, in music, in design, in ideas. Together, they began to design clothing that reflected their mutual interests and talent for provocation, beginning with the Teddy Boy style, but soon evolving into an edgier, rock 'n' roll look inspired by biker gear, then pivoting to selling rubber, leather and latex clothing borrowed from underground fetish scenes. All of these influences coalesced to create a movement that would define a generation: the phenomenon of punk rock. Although their paths eventually diverged, Malcolm and Vivienne's working relationship – which lasted from 1970 until 1983 – had an impact that is still being felt today. 'Malcolm's a one-off', Vivienne once said. 'He was fascinating and mad, and it was as though I was a coin and he showed me the other side.'

is for
NOSTALGIA OF MUD

In 1982, *The New York Times* wrote a scathing review of Vivienne Westwood's latest collection: 'Her show was full of frantic movements and squalid clothes. Petticoats made of sheet rock and bras worn over T-shirts were not amusing. The theme was "mud" and it was appropriate.' *The Times* may not have got it, but plenty of other people were galvanised by what Vivienne and Malcolm had created – it was unlike anything else at Fashion Week. The collection was inspired by costumes and cultures far from London, such as the traditional clothing of Peru and Bolivia. Models wore sheepskin jackets, fabric-covered boots, tattered, body-obscuring layers and oversized felt 'Mountain' hats, and danced down the catwalk to Appalachian folk music. One of the most memorable outfits saw a bra layered over a T-shirt, inspired by documentary photos of tribal woman who wore their bras visibly as status symbols – Vivienne's version was a bronze-coloured satin 1950s-style bra that was worn outside a tunic. Malcolm cannily dubbed the look 'underwear as outerwear.'

Significantly, Vivienne looked to traditional costume as it was still worn in Peru rather than to obsolete folk or peasant costume. It wasn't about appropriation, but a recognition of something powerful and pivotal.

With *Nostalgia of Mud* (A/W 1982–83), Vivienne and Malcolm's aim was 'to show in clothes and music that, in the post-industrial age, the roots of our culture lie in primitive societies,' as Malcolm put it.

Nostalgia of Mud

Nostalgia of Mud was also the name of a concept store that Vivienne and Malcolm had for a time in central London. The interior of the store resembled an archaeological dig, scaffolding surrounded the exterior, while inside a brown tarpaulin was stretched across the ceiling and clothing hung on rusty poles. It was intended to be equal parts impressive and intimidating: 'These shops were beautiful stage sets and never designed to sell anything,' said Malcolm.

In 2014, rapper and producer Pharrell Williams attended the Grammys sporting an Adidas track jacket, blue jeans and the Mountain Hat – which immediately went viral online. Proof that Vivienne was, once again, miles ahead of the curve.

The 'underwear as outerwear' trend was subsequently picked up by Jean-Paul Gaultier who commercialised the look and created Madonna's famous pointy bustier of her 1989 'Blond Ambition' tour.

The Mountain Hat became a staple of the Vivienne Westwood range and was repeated seasonally across the years.

is also for

New Romantics

Vivienne Westwood and Malcolm McLaren were instrumental in creating the aesthetic of the New Romantics – the poetic, historical, flamboyant style that defined the early 1980s. Vivienne's inspirations were the pirate as a romantic hero, the primitive style of the North American Indians and early 19th-century French aristocrats who scandalised Paris by wearing dresses and tunics modelled after ancient Greek and Roman dress. The look was taken up by musicians like Adam Ant and Boy George, who encapsulated the subversive androgyny of the period. 'Vivienne is constantly innovating, but her work during the punk and New Romantic periods defined the era,' John Galliano once said. 'It's impossible to think of the bands, the music and the spirit of both punk and the New Romantics without Vivienne's work.'

...

Gary Ness

Vivienne Westwood had a variety of mentors during her life, but none had such an impact on her creative life than Gary Ness. Gary was an artist, historian and aesthete, who adored history and introduced Vivienne to artists, philosophers and thinkers who would come to shape her collections. She described their relationship as 'like a wonderful school … whatever I'm interested in, Gary has a book on it, or will find a painting or a poem on a related theme.' Vivienne once said, 'The biggest influence on my life bar none was Gary Ness. I would not be the person I am if I had not met him.'

O

is also for

Orb

The symbol that represents the Vivienne Westwood label is instantly recognisable – an orb encircled, Saturn-like, by a ring. It was based on the orb logo of the heritage British brand Harris Tweed, which Vivienne appropriated for herself when she presented her collection of the same name. For Vivienne, the logo perfectly encapsulated her respect for history and heritage as well as her knack for creation and innovation, with the royal orb representing tradition and the Saturn rings representing the future. Its regal connotations were not by chance either: 'Of course I've often, just peripherally, been associated with the Queen, as in "Queen of Punk",' she said. Today, the orb logo is iconic and synonymous with the Westwood brand.

...

Optimism

Vivienne Westwood's activism was based on a sense of urgency that humanity was running out of time. She was appalled by the inaction of leaders and governments when it came to things like addressing climate change and overconsumption, and disturbed by the myriad of human rights issues she saw unfolding every day. In spite of this, Vivienne held out hope for the future. 'We're born with optimism, aren't we?' she once told *Purple* magazine. 'Most people are optimistic, and this is probably one of the problems. But you have to behave as if there is still a chance to do something. And what you can do today is so much better than what you can do tomorrow. It's very urgent!'

Although many members of the fashion press were baffled by the outlandish silhouette, Vivienne loved it. 'It's a question of adjusting your eyes,' she said. 'It's only perverse because it's unexpected.'

Vivienne cast top models like Kate Moss, Nadja Auermann, Naomi Campbell, Linda Evangelista, Helena Christensen and Christy Turlington in the show. They walked the runway to audible cheers, cat-calls and wolf-whistles from the audience.

Filmmaker Mike Figgis, who shot a documentary on the *On Liberty* show, remembered how the models responded to wearing Vivienne's designs: 'She's inviting them to be very strong about their bodies and sexuality, to feel good and powerful in her clothes – extravagant and flamboyant.'

The Italian supermodel Carla Bruni wore one of the collection's most memorable looks: an opulent faux-fur coat, which she threw open to reveal that she was wearing nothing underneath bar a matching fur thong.

is for

ON LIBERTY

Named after an essay by the philosopher John Stuart Mill, *On Liberty* (A/W 1994–95) was an ode to a particularly Westwood kind of femininity. Championing the voluptuousness of the female form, Vivienne created a collection that played with proportion by way of bustles and padding – and transformed supermodels from lithe to curvaceous. This new silhouette, with its cushioned bum-pad, was designed to make the waist look tiny by comparison, while exceptionally high platform stilettos lengthened the legs and made the body sway. This bold silhouette was intended as a body-positive statement and a critique on the trend that prized waif-like physiques. 'I happen to think that a lady is the most beautiful creature in the whole world,' said Vivienne at the time. 'I think it's natural that she should want to augment this potential; I think it's natural she should stand on high heels and therefore ... all the bumps and curves of her beautiful physique come into play.'

is for PROTEST

Protest was in Vivienne Westwood's blood. Her strong sense of social justice, her commitment to her ideals, and her unwavering dedication that fashion was as worthy a place to discuss politics and ideas as a classroom or town hall – these were the things that shaped her work and her life. Punk was a protest, taking aim at middle-class values and flying in the face of taboos – but as time went on, she became more politically engaged with issues around climate change, animal rights, ethical labour, sustainability and nuclear disarmament. In one memorable protest, Vivienne drove a tank through the streets of Oxfordshire to the home of the British prime minister of the time, David Cameron, to protest against the environmentally disastrous practice of fracking (extracting gas by drilling into subterranean rock). From the catwalk to the streets, Vivienne used her platform to make her voice heard: she supported environmental organisations like Cool Earth, the Environmental Justice Foundation and Friends of the Earth, was an ambassador for Greenpeace, and spearheaded a global campaign to stop drilling and industrial fishing in the Arctic. She fought the good fight and demanded that others follow her lead: 'I want you to help me save the world,' she said. 'I can't do it on my own.'

is also for

"I am Julian Assange."

In 2014, Vivienne shaved off her hair. The move was a calculated one to attract the media's attention – and then make everyone sit up and listen. Shortly after making the change, she gave an interview in which she announced she was downsizing her clothing empire in a bid to promote environmental sustainability and encouraged people to consume less: 'Buy less, choose well, make it last.'

Vivienne had a particular interest in drawing attention to political dissidents and whistle-blowers – such as Julian Assange, Chelsea Manning and Leonard Peltier – whose activities made them political prisoners and she campaigned tirelessly to raise awareness about their plight.

When it came to protest, Vivienne believed everyone had a role to play: 'It's a war for the very existence of the human race. And that of the planet,' she said.

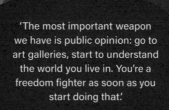

'The most important weapon we have is public opinion: go to art galleries, start to understand the world you live in. You're a freedom fighter as soon as you start doing that.'

Pirate

'I wanted that rakish look of clothes which didn't fit,' said Vivienne of the *Pirate* collection (A/W 1981–82). For her catwalk debut, she drew on the historical dress of highwaymen, dandies, buccaneers and pirates, with an emphasis on billowing, oversized shapes. The mostly non-professional models strutted the runway in outfits they'd selected for themselves. 'The hobo, the pirate, the punk rocker – they're all the same,' Vivienne said. 'They're all part of the dispossessed, defying laws and creating their own.'

...

Punkature

Punkature (S/S 1983) looked towards the future while drawing from the past: it featured images from the movie *Blade Runner* paired with toile de jouy prints, distressed fabrics fastened with buttons made from tin-can lids, folkwear-inspired silhouettes and stretchy tube skirts made from cotton stockinette. With its name a mash-up of punk and couture, this collection pushed Vivienne's creativity in a bold new direction.

...

Portrait

'I wanted the look of a model who'd just stepped out of a portrait,' said Vivienne of her A/W 1990–91 range. The mood was one of sensuality and opulence, drawing inspiration from the world of 18th-century oil paintings. Models wore gold-embossed velvet bodysuits, aristocratic hunting jackets and opulent furs. Jeans, T-shirts and the Stature of Liberty corset (one of Vivienne's most sought-after designs) were emblazoned with photographic prints of François Boucher paintings.

Q

is also for

Quotes

Vivienne Westwood had a way with words, swinging from grand pronouncements to Zen-like koans. She was a rare public figure who was almost totally unguarded in interviews and happily aired her opinions – no matter who might be offended. Her quotes on fashion provide a snapshot into her unique perspective: 'Fashion is about eventually being naked,' she once said. And on another occasion: 'Fashion is the passing of time.' And her most remembered saying? 'You have a much better life if you wear impressive clothes.'

...

Queer

Vivienne Westwood's clothing has always held appeal to the queer community – whether it was the leathermen and sex workers who flocked to SEX in the 1970s or the gender-fluid youth of today who see themselves reflected in Andreas Kronthaler's creations. In 2013, Vivienne and Malcolm's bondage pants and gay cowboy T-shirt were included in the exhibition *A Queer History of Fashion: From the Closet to the Catwalk*, recognising that their deliberate association with so-called 'deviant' sexualities had given queer youth of the era an important avenue for self-expression. For Vivienne, clothing was inextricably linked to the creation of identity – and a powerful tool for anyone whose identities were rejected or repressed by the mainstream. 'You've only got to think of cross-dressing – e.g. women wearing tailored suits – to see how clothes help you to play a role, to see that clothes have the effect of giving you a role,' she said. A style maven, iconoclast and provocateur, Vivienne will always be an icon for the queer community.

Ten years after the Sex Pistols' sang their anti-establishment anthem 'God Save the Queen', Vivienne showed a collection that drew on classic British style and the clothes of the royal family – the collection even included a range of faux-ermine capes and crowns fashioned from fabric.

Throughout her entire career, Vivienne could never quite shake off her early reputation, something that both amused and annoyed her: 'I am a very nice woman, and very easy to work with,' she once said. 'But I am always known as the Queen of Punk.'

In 1985, Vivienne was asked whose style she most admired. Her response? 'The Queen. I love clothes that make you look rich, not showy ... The Queen looked wonderfully sexy in her coronation pictures by Cecil Beaton, and she is the epitome of '80s elegance. She has stood still for so long in the security of her own chic that she is now utterly stylish.'

In 1992, Queen Elizabeth II awarded Vivienne the Order of the British Empire – and to the astonishment of some, she accepted the honour. Vivienne issued a press release to explain that she was no longer interested in attacking the establishment because she was concerned with 'something more fundamental – the concept of civilisation itself.' Besides, she said, 'it's good for business.'

Of the crown she designed, Vivienne said: 'It's comic but it's terribly chic. I like to keep it on when I'm having dinner – like ladies who keep their coats on to take tea. It's so English, yet terribly attractive.'

is for

THE QUEEN

She may have been a Dame on paper, but Vivienne Westwood was, and always will be, the Queen of Punk. The idea of feminine power – sexually, politically or otherwise – was a constant source of inspiration and this often played out through references to royalty in her collections, whether that was her own take on the red hunting jackets worn by the British aristocracy, mining Tudor styles like the ruff, or use of the crinoline skirt for a modern outlook on royal styles from the past. Queen Elizabeth II was a potent symbol throughout Vivienne's work – sometimes as a figure to be mocked and sometimes as a figure to be emulated. In the early days, Vivienne and Malcolm McLaren scandalised the British establishment by producing T-shirts printed with a swastika, an inverted crucifix, a postage stamp featuring Queen Elizabeth's unmistakable profile, and the word DESTROY scrawled over the top. This was swiftly followed by a T-shirt that stuck a safety pin through the lip of the monarch – turning her from prim to punk. Vivienne saw this as an affectionate gesture, as though putting a safety pin in her lips suggested that the Queen could be one of them.

is for

ROCKING HORSE SHOES

Comprised of a thick wooden sole with a slightly tapered front and a nick in the back of the heel, Vivienne Westwood's rocking horse shoe is one of her most recognisable designs. Vivienne debuted the style in her *Harris Tweed* collection (A/W 1987–88), in an era when other designers were showing neat, flat ballet pumps, classic court shoes or trainers. But Vivienne was, as always, marching to the beat of her own drum – or in this case, rocking to the beat of her own drum. Their name was derived from the rocking motion the wearer had to adopt in order to negotiate walking safely in them, as the wooden platforms had absolutely no flexibility. Wearing them meant a change in your entire posture, with the unique design bestowing poise and elevation, as well as movement. 'I wanted these little childish shoes, like sandals but a bit like clogs,' Vivienne recalled. 'They had to have a little platform – they rocked a bit.'

Beginning with the *Portrait* collection (A/W 1990–91), Vivienne began putting her models in enormously elevated platform shoes.

When it came to shoes, Vivienne was an innovator right from the start. For the *Witches* collection (A/W 1983–84), she put models in custom-made triple-tongue trainers, inspired by New York hip-hop culture – making her arguably the first designer to put sneakers on the catwalk.

'Before me, platforms and heels were always added to the shoe, like a separate support,' Vivienne said. 'I've taken the leather or fabric over the whole edifice, shoe and platform. It's a simple thing but makes them radically more beautiful: an extension of the whole look, and the leg. I'd order leather to cover right down the platform, so it looked a bit orthopaedic, as well – a bit kinky. They have become a classic.'

Recalling both the ancient Venetian chopine shoe and the Japanese geta or okobo sandal, the rocking horse shoe quite literally puts its wearers on a pedestal.

'I love to put women on a pedestal and give them these high-heeled shoes,' said Vivienne. 'And that's why I invented the platforms, and that's why they took on the particular form that they did, because I wanted it to be like a pedestal.'

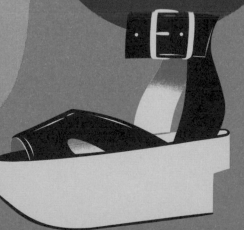

is also for

Rebellion

Vivienne Westwood's name may be synonymous with punk, but for her, real rebellion lay beyond punk's anarchic ethos. 'They liked to look great and run around, but it wasn't enough,' she explained. 'It's not enough to destroy. You have to have ideas.' For Vivienne, rebellion came through education. It was only through studying the greatest minds of the past that you could come to break free of the establishment and orthodoxy. Vivienne wanted to inspire people to become activists, like she was – to make change by taking real-world action.

...

Red Label

Vivienne Westwood Red Label was launched in 1999 as a more affordable prêt-a-porter line to complement the existing demi-couture range shown on runways. This was later supplemented by Vivienne Westwood Man and Anglomania, a mass-market diffusion line. For a time, Vivienne was designing six shows a year – two Gold Label, two Red Label and two menswear. Later, she made the decision to scale things back, in line with her environmental concerns around overconsumption. 'I'm trying to completely reduce the scale of operation,' she said in 2014. 'I'm concentrating on quality, not quantity.' Although she was in the business of selling clothes, she used her platform to encourage people to shop less. 'I just think people should invest in the world. Don't invest in fashion, but invest in the world.'

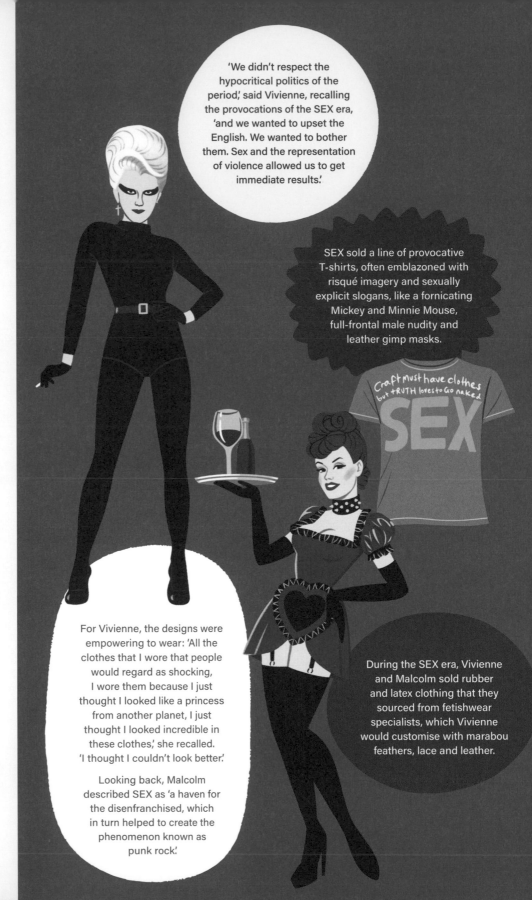

S

is also for

The Swire Family

Vivienne Westwood was born to Gordon and Dora Swire in 1941, the first of their three children. The family was solidly working class: Gordon worked as a fruiterer and later ran a post office, while Dora worked in the cotton mills. Although a little conservative, they were supportive of their oldest daughter. When asked about Vivienne in an interview, Dora said: 'When she was a girl she was like she is now, only small. She's become cleverer. She was always stubborn, inquisitive and bossy. I have two other children, just as important.'

...

Seditionaries

In 1977, Vivienne Westwood and Malcolm McLaren shuttered SEX and re-opened it as Seditionaries: Clothes for Heroes. It supplied the punk movement with its distinctive look: bondage trousers, ripped muslin shirts held together with safety pins, T-shirts printed with a confronting mix of slogans, symbols and imagery – including the newly minted anarchist symbol, a capital A scrawled within a circle. Vivienne chose the name as a call to arms, saying that the word 'always meant, to me, the necessity to seduce people into revolt.'

...

Sara Stockbridge

It's difficult to imagine the Vivienne Westwood woman without thinking of Sara Stockbridge. With her pin-up-girl looks, platinum blonde hair and English rose complexion, she was the ideal Westwood woman. 'She's totally uninhibited,' said Vivienne of her muse. 'I love the way she moves. Just like a real old stripper, and yet very classy-looking.'

'We didn't respect the hypocritical politics of the period,' said Vivienne, recalling the provocations of the SEX era, 'and we wanted to upset the English. We wanted to bother them. Sex and the representation of violence allowed us to get immediate results.'

SEX sold a line of provocative T-shirts, often emblazoned with risqué imagery and sexually explicit slogans, like a fornicating Mickey and Minnie Mouse, full-frontal male nudity and leather gimp masks.

For Vivienne, the designs were empowering to wear: 'All the clothes that I wore that people would regard as shocking, I wore them because I just thought I looked like a princess from another planet, I just thought I looked incredible in these clothes,' she recalled. 'I thought I couldn't look better.'

Looking back, Malcolm described SEX as 'a haven for the disenfranchised, which in turn helped to create the phenomenon known as punk rock.'

During the SEX era, Vivienne and Malcolm sold rubber and latex clothing that they sourced from fetishwear specialists, which Vivienne would customise with marabou feathers, lace and leather.

is for

SEX

In 1974, Vivienne Westwood and Malcolm McLaren changed the name of their King's Road boutique to its most provocative name yet: SEX. 'England is the home of the flasher, we're all closet perverts,' mused Malcolm, and the two of them set about creating a space where perversions of all kinds could flourish. The words 'Craft must have clothes but truth loves to go naked' was scrawled above the door. The interior was sprayed with pornographic graffiti, hung with rubber curtains and stocked with latex and leather clothing, and kink-friendly accessories like padlocks, chains, whips and handcuffs.

It was a store designed to intimidate, and consequently it attracted a certain kind of customer: voyeurs and flashers, dominatrices and sex workers, celebrities, revolutionaries and the rebellious youth. The store was the epicentre of a new movement bubbling up from the streets, which rejected puritanism, authority and middle-class values, and set about creating a whole new way of living.

Tartan is a fabric with a long and illustrious history dating back to the 1600s, when Scottish Highlanders used dyes made from plants, roots, berries and trees to colour wool and weave it into unique patterns. Over time, these patterns came to represent a symbol of a specific geographical area and clan kinship, and became intimately interwoven with politics, pride, protest and rebellion – ideas that resonated with Vivienne Westwood in the 1970s. At the time, she and Malcolm were producing their infamous bondage suits in shiny black sateen, replete with silver zips and straps that trussed the legs together. Vivienne made a version in a beautiful wool tartan – both she and Malcolm wore versions of the look in press photographs, while punk icon Jordan Mooney was known to wear a mini tartan kilt as part of her outrageous work wardrobe at the King's Road boutique. The fabric soon became a punk staple, used to signify a new kind of clan membership and representative of the mood of dissent and opposition that was bubbling up from the streets. But this was only the beginning of Vivienne's love affair with tartan – later, it became a signature of her label, used in every garment imaginable, from hats to corsets to sweeping ballgowns.

is for

TARTAN

At a time when other designers were trying to revive punk, Vivienne used tartan to evoke unadulterated glamour. She had tartans sewn into bustle-backed skirts, nipped-in-waist jackets, chic trouser suits, and showstopping evening gowns crafted from tartan taffeta.

One of Vivienne's favourite effects was to use different tartans in the same outfit, layering checks both vertically and horizontally to achieve an overload of pattern.

Why did tartan become synonymous with punk? Vivienne's genius was to recognise that the fabric was already a loaded historical symbol of repression and resistance within the British national story, an emblem of the Scots' struggle against the authority of the throne. When used to create outlandish garments that made people point and snicker in the street, Vivienne proclaimed tartan as the fabric of disenfranchised youth and a rebellion against the system. Those associations have never gone away.

In the 1990s, Vivienne experimented with using tartan to different effects – in the *Anglomania* collection (A/W 1993–94), for example, she drew on the fabric's heritage as a material loved by British aristocracy.

'Every fabric that you look at in England has a charge of content,' she once stated – and few fabrics offered a richer tapestry of inspiration than tartan.

is also for

Too Fast to Live, Too Young to Die
In 1973, Vivienne Westwood and Malcolm McLaren changed the name of their King's Road boutique to Too Fast to Live, Too Young to Die. They were no longer interested in the Ted look – it was all about rockers. They sold T-shirts customised with studs or sewn with chicken bones spelling out PERV, ROCK and SCUM, alongside leather jackets and vintage Levi's. This harder-edged look, built around black, leather, chains and studs, led them towards an increasingly fetish-inspired aesthetic.

...

Thomas Tew
The figure of the pirate served as a touchstone for Vivienne Westwood throughout her career, both as sartorial inspiration and as a romantic ideal. Thomas Tew, one of the most notorious sea outlaws of the 17th century, claimed a special place in the Westwood universe, after Vivienne and Malcolm adopted his flag – a crooked arm holding a short scimitar sword – as the logo for the Worlds End label.

...

Time Machine
Vivienne Westwood's heroine for her A/W 1988–89 collection was Miss Marple, the crime-solving spinster of Agatha Christie's novels. The show opened with models in prim Harris Tweed suits sexed up with ruffled petticoats and platform shoes, and featured Fair Isle sweaters with computer game patterns, schoolboy-style blazers, and jerkins inspired by medieval armour. Halfway through the show, dancer Michael Clark performed the Ghillie Callum, a Scottish folk dance, in full Highland regalia.

U *is also for*

Unreliable Narrator

Like any good fable, Vivienne Westwood's story has many versions. For many years, Malcolm McLaren's version of the birth of punk rock, in which he was the genius and Vivienne merely his faithful handmaiden, was taken as gospel. After their romantic relationship collapsed, Malcolm had no qualms about giving interviews to the press that painted Vivienne in an unflattering light and diminished her role in their creative partnership – he said that she was 'never a creative thinker, never an innovator' and even went so far as to claim that she would still be a primary school teacher if it wasn't for him. After Malcolm's death in 2010, Vivienne went on to release her memoir, co-written with actor and biographer Ian Kelly, which told her side of the story. 'Malcolm's dead, and I can actually say things I wouldn't have said if he'd been alive,' she said in an interview with *W Magazine*. 'I have such a loyalty to Malcolm, even though he was so horrible.' Of course, like many people touched by genius, Vivienne was also prone to myth-making, liable to exaggerate, and entirely incapable of seeing things from anyone's perspective but her own. Although she was often characterised in the media as an eccentric personality who spoke in grand pronouncements and cryptic riddles, she was certainly aware of the power of a self-fashioned narrative and being the owner of her own story: 'Everybody knows that their past life is like a series of different little scenes,' she once said. 'It's a story and you've selected from your memory the things that you think are important. Nothing from the past is entirely true.'

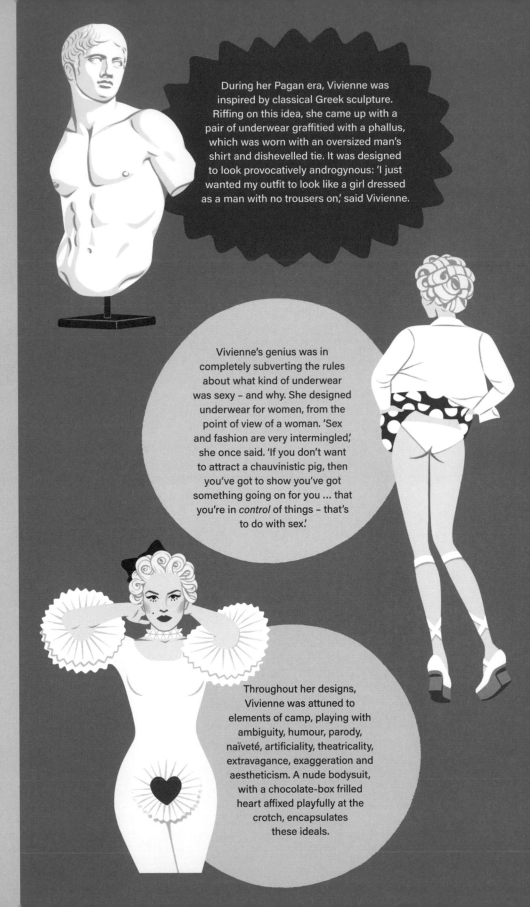

During her Pagan era, Vivienne was inspired by classical Greek sculpture. Riffing on this idea, she came up with a pair of underwear graffitied with a phallus, which was worn with an oversized man's shirt and dishevelled tie. It was designed to look provocatively androgynous: 'I just wanted my outfit to look like a girl dressed as a man with no trousers on,' said Vivienne.

Vivienne's genius was in completely subverting the rules about what kind of underwear was sexy – and why. She designed underwear for women, from the point of view of a woman. 'Sex and fashion are very intermingled,' she once said. 'If you don't want to attract a chauvinistic pig, then you've got to show you've got something going on for you ... that you're in *control* of things – that's to do with sex.'

Throughout her designs, Vivienne was attuned to elements of camp, playing with ambiguity, humour, parody, naïveté, artificiality, theatricality, extravagance, exaggeration and aestheticism. A nude bodysuit, with a chocolate-box frilled heart affixed playfully at the crotch, encapsulates these ideals.

'Andreas always changes his underwear according to what he's wearing,' Vivienne Westwood said in a 2009 interview with *The Guardian*. 'Whereas I don't bother wearing any these days.' In fact, it seemed she rarely bothered to wear underwear – a fact that was made obvious in 1992 when she twirled for the cameras after receiving her OBE and revealed a distinct lack of knickers. In spite of her personal ambivalence to the practice, creating innovative, irreverent underwear was part of Vivienne's personal fashion vocabulary. She pioneered underwear as outerwear, transformed the corset into a modern fashion icon, and delighted in the subversive potential of any garment that was meant to stay hidden. One of her most memorable designs consisted of flesh-coloured stockings appliquéd with a strategically placed fig leaf – a witty riff on the Garden of Eden and pagan sensuality. The fashion media at the time called them unwearable, uncommercial and vulgar ... not that it mattered a bit to Vivienne. 'When I first did the fig leaf in 1989, I just kept screaming,' she said. 'It was so porno and so hilariously mad. Then I got used to it, and I think it looks so elegant and ironic.' Vivienne liked to wear hers as in the *Voyage to Cythera* (A/W 1989–90) collection – with a neat shirt and riding jacket, paired with rocking horse shoes.

U *is for*

UNDERWEAR

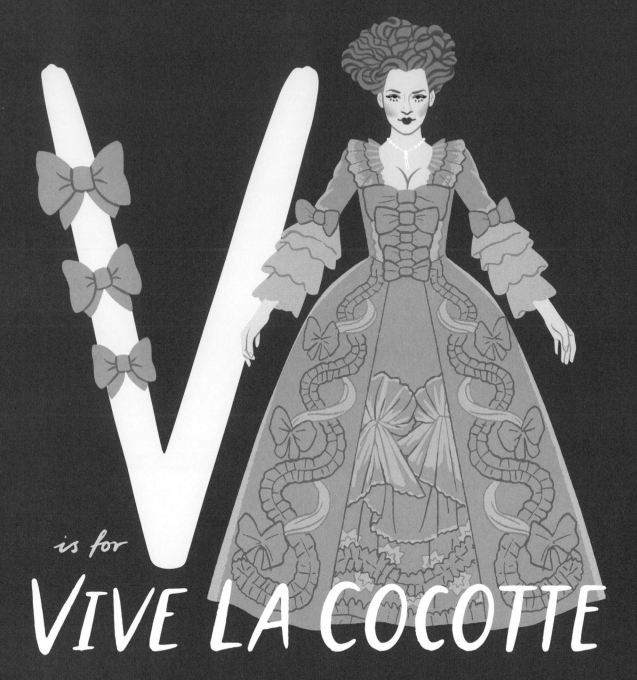

V is for VIVE LA COCOTTE

Vivienne Westwood understood coquetry. In her *Vive la Cocotte* collection (A/W 1995–96), she reinforced her reputation for creating clothes with a uniquely feminine sexual charge, with outfits that exaggerated the figure through the use of bustles and padding. The result was an outrageously hourglass shape that didn't rely on corsetry (although, being Vivienne, there were a few of those too). A parade of bosomy, bustled ladies in six-inch-heeled boots, tight button-front knits, wench dresses, opulent faux furs and saucy tweed suits rounded out Vivienne's ode to the inherent beauty of the female form. In the programme notes, Vivienne wrote: 'It is clear that this return to formality in dress is a reaction against the sloppy mediocrity of our age.' As with the *Dressing Up* collection (A/W 1991–92) of a few years earlier, the collection suggested that a more beautiful, more heroic, more extraordinary way of dressing could endow its wearer with a better – or at least a more interesting – life.

Looking back over her career, Vivienne would often refer to *Vive la Cocotte* as her favourite collection.

With its luxurious fabrics, couture constructions and provocative silhouettes that pushed the boundaries of acceptability, *Vive la Cocotte* was a culmination of Vivienne's entire career. She described it as 'almost a fusion of SEX and Harris Tweed' – an inspired blend of historical dress and kink.

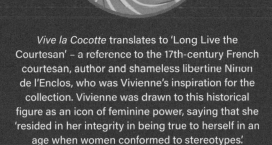

Vive la Cocotte translates to 'Long Live the Courtesan' – a reference to the 17th-century French courtesan, author and shameless libertine Ninon de l'Enclos, who was Vivienne's inspiration for the collection. Vivienne was drawn to this historical figure as an icon of feminine power, saying that she 'resided in her integrity in being true to herself in an age when women conformed to stereotypes'.

Although Vivienne was committed to her new silhouette, the collection was considered so unwearable that she ended up making two entirely separate ranges – the catwalk collection in all its architectural glory and a more toned-down range that was sold in stores. Vivienne, of course, wore the catwalk versions with flair.

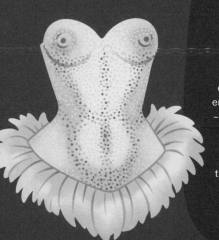

is also for

Voyage to Cythera
Inspired by pagan sensuality filtered through the lens of French classical art, *Voyage to Cythera* (A/W 1989–90) saw Savile Row–style tailored jackets teamed with flesh-coloured leggings affixed with Perspex fig leaves over the pubis, harlequin-inspired bodysuits and mini-crini dresses worn with commedia dell'arte masks. The fig-leaf tights caused an immediate sensation. 'It's very difficult to come up with something shocking and original,' she said. 'I surprised myself by making a garment that shocked me.'

...

Vive la Bagatelle
For S/S 1997, Vivienne Westwood was in a flirtatious mood. The *Vive la Bagatelle* woman sashayed down the runway in waist-enhancing dresses, puff-sleeved blouses and narrow pencil skirts, divine corsets and spectacular ballgowns. The mood of the collection was one of decorative femininity – 'It's about flirting ... a trifle, a nothing, a ribbon; a bow tied prettily and easily undone,' read the programme.

...

Vegetarianism
Vivienne was a vegetarian for much of her life. It was a choice that made sense to her both financially and ethically – raised during the post-war years, austerity came as second nature to her. 'I cooked macrobiotically, just rice, vegetables and a few nuts,' she remembered. Dedicated to protecting the planet's animal life, she appeared in a PETA campaign, banned the use of fur in her collections, and used her runway shows to protest against factory farming.

is also for

Witches

Inspired by the work of graffiti artist Keith Haring, the African voodoo tradition and hip-hop culture in New York, *Witches* (A/W 1983–84) was an innovative, primal collection. Models danced down the runway in wool capes with peaked hoods, clingy tube skirts, oversized shearling jackets and sporty sweats worn with triple-tongued trainers. *Witches* was the last collection that Vivienne Westwood co-designed with Malcolm McLaren – after it, they parted ways, both professionally and romantically.

...

Worlds End

The King's Road boutique went through many names, but its most enduring is Worlds End. Originally named to coincide with the launch of the *Pirate* collection, the boutique had sloping floors and tiny windows, meant to evoke the feeling of being on a galleon ship. A large clock affixed to the exterior of the store displayed 13 hours, with its hands travelling backwards. Today, Worlds End is still a mecca for Westwood fans.

...

Ben Westwood

Vivienne Westwood's relationship with her oldest son was a sometimes rocky one. She split up with his father, Derek Westwood, when Ben was a toddler, so he spent much of his childhood with his maternal grandparents. As an adult, Ben became an erotic photographer – his mother, perhaps surprisingly, seemed to not entirely approve. After reconciling with Vivienne in his mid-40s, he went on to launch his own fashion line. He appeared in the A/W 2023–24 Andreas Kronthaler for Vivienne Westwood campaign as a tribute to his late mother.

The common thread running through Vivienne's career was a commitment to elevating women through dress: 'I think my clothes are extremely heroic,' she said. 'I like to make women feel and look important. I do believe that people need power as much as they need love.'

Vivienne was interested in making clothes for women who didn't conform to society's ideals – women whose bodies were not necessarily waifishly thin or sculpted and gym-toned. 'I don't understand why people keep plugging this boring asexual body,' she said. 'At my age I'd rather have a bit of flab, I actually think that's more sexy. I *like* my own body.'

'Of course fashion is frivolous. It *should* be!' she once said. 'It has to be to be seductive. A woman's power lies in coquetry.'

In Westwood clothing, a woman could feel dashing and heroic or coquettish and seductive. She could feel like a goddess or a monster. She could wear men's clothing in a feminine way. She could be entirely herself.

Vivienne understood that women looked to clothing as a way of asserting their personality, their sexuality and their power – and that those who dismissed fashion as merely frivolous were missing the point.

W is for

WOMEN

What do women want? For Vivienne Westwood, the answer was obvious: women want to feel beautiful and powerful – or, in her preferred vocabulary, heroic. She made clothes that would endow a woman with a sense of confidence and sexuality derived from how they made her *feel*, rather than what they made her look like. 'I'm not interested in clothing a perfect body,' Vivienne once declared. 'People with perfect bodies make me suspicious about what's in their heads.' The women she surrounded herself with – from her 'shop-girl goddesses' Jordan Mooney and Chrissie Hynde to her favourite models, like Sara Stockbridge and Susie Bick – exemplified these traits. Her designs redefined what was sexy – whether that was the provocation of a rubber dress from SEX, the billowing layers of the *Pirate* collection (A/W 1981–82), the subversive properness of *Harris Tweed* (A/W 1987–88), or the erotic revelry of the Pagan years.

X

is for

X-RATED

'I have an in-built perversity,' Vivienne Westwood once said, 'a kind of in-built clock which always reacts against anything orthodox.' This impetus to shock and agitate seemed to be sometimes deliberate and sometimes merely a side effect of being Vivienne – she could cause a furore without really trying. A case in point was her infamous twirl for the cameras after receiving her OBE. It wasn't that she meant to cause a national incident by meeting the Queen without her underwear on – that was just how she dressed. She saw no issue with being photographed nude by Juergen Teller when she was in her late 60s and was unconcerned by the feverish reaction to the photos in the tabloid press. For Vivienne, each scandal she caused simply reaffirmed her commitment to challenging the status quo: 'My job is always to confront the Establishment to try and find out where freedom lies and what you can do,' she said.

In 1975, SEX offered a T-shirt designed by Malcolm McLaren showing two cowboys, naked from the waist down, with their penises nearly touching. The first customer to wear it in public was immediately arrested. Within 24 hours, the boutique was raided for indecency and Malcolm was prosecuted under the obscenity laws for 'exposing to public view an indecent exhibition.'

Other T-shirts were emblazoned with equally provocative imagery: a naked black footballer, a leather gimp mask like the one worn by a serial rapist who was stalking the city of Cambridge at the time, a troubling image of a shirtless 12-year-old boy smoking a cigarette.

Another shirt featured a close-up photograph of a pair of female breasts, printed to be placed at breast height on the wearer – the effect was androgynous and strangely unsettling.

Vivienne never lost her taste for challenging puritanism and had a knack for playing with distinctly British hang-ups, like anxieties around nudity. She sometimes sent models down the catwalk half-dressed – in *Café Society* (S/S 1994), for example, Kate Moss memorably wore nothing but a mini skirt and orb necklace, accessorised with a tricorn hat and a Magnum ice cream.

is also for

Xerox

Collage, bricolage and montage were part of the visual language of the punk movement – known in the 1970s as 'Xerox art'. The Xerox photocopier helped build the DIY movement, making fanzines possible and helping to establish copying and reproduction as legitimate forms of art (as Andy Warhol had also demonstrated). It also gave rise to a particularly punk aesthetic – hand-written captions, typewriter headlines, montage graphics – that Vivienne and Malcolm used in the SEX and Seditionaries clothing. It was an aesthetic that delighted in repurposed imagery, decontextualised slogans and shocking juxtapositions. While Vivienne eventually evolved her visual language beyond the cheap thrills of Xerox art, she never lost her respect for copying as a legitimate practice.

She believed that fashion was based on renewal and reinvention, yet the only way to innovate was to look backwards: 'When you look into the past, you start to see the standards of excellence, the good taste in the way things were done, put together, formed,' she said. 'By trying to copy technique, you build up your own technique.' She was one of the first modern-day designers to exactly copy the cut and construction of historical dress – thus revolutionising fashion for today. Her knack for innovation and for changing the direction of fashion also meant she was one of the most copied designers – not just by high-street stores but by other designers. Vivienne was fairly unfazed by this: 'It has always been the case that when others have copied me they lifted me up with them,' she said. 'I never begrudge people copying me – as long as they don't mess it up.'

is also for

Youth Culture

Vivienne Westwood's genius was rarely born from being attuned to the shifting currents of youth culture – that was Malcolm McLaren's talent. Malcolm liked to co-opt things: he had a way of sensing trends that were bubbling up from the street and knowing how to market them. Vivienne was less keyed in to youth culture. Aside from an affection for the fashion and music of the 1950s – the era in which she herself came of age – she tended to ignore contemporary culture entirely. She never watched television, despised fashion magazines, and couldn't care less what was going on in popular culture (she often relied on her husband Andreas and younger members of her design team to inform her as to what was going on with the youth). Instead, she found inspiration from the past and the geniuses who had come before her, mining the vast archives of history for things that she could look at with a fresh perspective and make anew. Her touchstones were high art and high culture, and she studied them like a student. It was this singular ability to be unswayed by trends that allowed her to create things that were truly new – that created the zeitgeist, rather than just leaching off it. For Vivienne, society's obsession with youth was something to be corrected, and the idea that artists were at their best in their youth was a foolish one: 'As for this romantic idea that an artist has all the fire in his youth, and then when they get old they become boring, it's just not true,' she said. Her own career was testament to this.

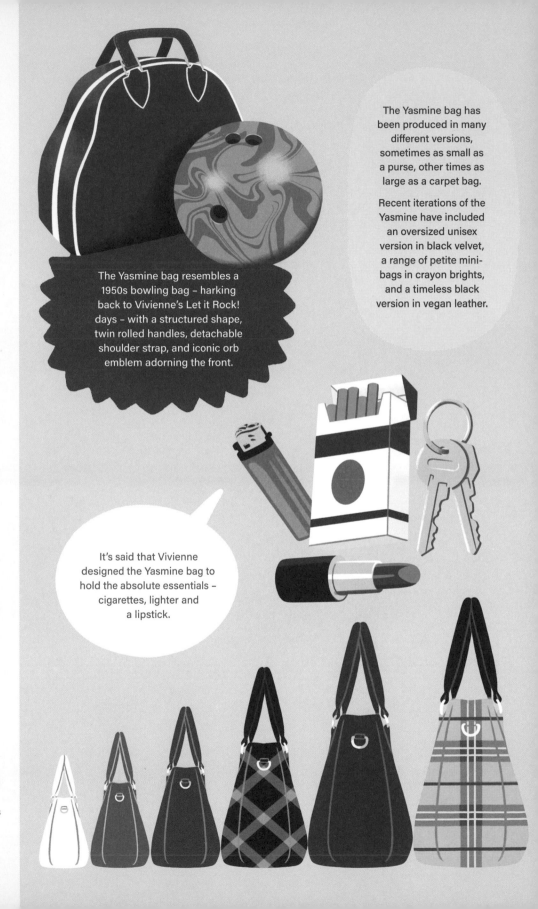

The Yasmine bag resembles a 1950s bowling bag – harking back to Vivienne's Let it Rock! days – with a structured shape, twin rolled handles, detachable shoulder strap, and iconic orb emblem adorning the front.

The Yasmine bag has been produced in many different versions, sometimes as small as a purse, other times as large as a carpet bag.

Recent iterations of the Yasmine have included an oversized unisex version in black velvet, a range of petite mini-bags in crayon brights, and a timeless black version in vegan leather.

It's said that Vivienne designed the Yasmine bag to hold the absolute essentials – cigarettes, lighter and a lipstick.

The Yasmine bag is one of Vivienne Westwood's most iconic pieces. Designed in the late-1980s and shown on the runway in collections like *Time Machine* (A/W 1988–89), *Café Society* (S/S 1994) and *Anglomania* (A/W 1993–94), Vivienne named the bag after the French designer Yasmine Eslami, who, like Sara Stockbridge and Susie Bick, was one of Vivienne's muses. Yasmine worked in Vivienne's design studio in the 1980s and '90s, doing everything from press to studio work to designing for Westwood's Red Label. 'When you come from school and it's your first job, it's like your family', she said. 'It was 24-hour Westwood world'. Her time with Vivienne in London left a lasting impact on her: 'The British are different; Vivienne is different', she said. 'In Paris, we're more conservative. In London, people don't care; there's not the same judgement as here'. After working with Vivienne for 10 years, she went on to become a stylist at *Purple* magazine and the artistic director at swimwear and beachwear house ERES. She launched her own lingerie label in 2010, simply called Yasmine Eslami. Yasmine maintained a connection to Vivienne long after she left the house – she has done several collaborations with Andreas Kronthaler on swimwear collections. And the bag that bears her name? It continues to be a staple of the Vivienne Westwood label today.

is for

YASMINE BAG

Z
is for

ZIPS

Punk style grew out of a melting pot of references, but its obsession with zips came straight from the fetish subculture. Vivienne Westwood began experimenting with zips in the SEX era, when she and Malcolm McLaren produced their seminal bondage collection in which garments were studded, buckled, strapped, rubberised, slit, shredded and chained, with zips everywhere that made them gape in unusual places, like the back of the legs. Designed to both shock and titillate, these garments could be kept chastely done up or unzipped to reveal flashes of flesh. Rather than being purely functional, zips were utilised as an aesthetic element that hinted at the possibility of being unzipped. Ripped from their functional use, zips took on a life of their own as punk's favourite accessory.

For Vivienne, zips, safety pins and razor blades were part of an anti-fashion scheme of adornment that nodded to cultures outside of the West, thereby questioning European cultural supremacy: 'Safety pins definitely had an analogy in Third World culture, like putting feathers in your hair ... or people in Africa who made necklaces out of old car hub caps.'

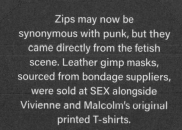

Zips may now be synonymous with punk, but they came directly from the fetish scene. Leather gimp masks, sourced from bondage suppliers, were sold at SEX alongside Vivienne and Malcolm's original printed T-shirts.

One of Vivienne's Too Fast to Live, Too Young to Die–era innovations was to slash open a T-shirt and insert zips over where the wearer's nipples would be. Instead of using the usual flat-end zipper, she opted for a ball-and-chain zipper, which dangled when you moved.

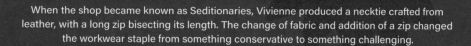

When the shop became known as Seditionaries, Vivienne produced a necktie crafted from leather, with a long zip bisecting its length. The change of fabric and addition of a zip changed the workwear staple from something conservative to something challenging.

Z is also for

Zoot Suit

Known for its broad shoulders, nipped waist and baggy pegged trousers, the zoot suit was a symbol of rebellion in the 1970s – a deliberately historical fashion choice that set its wearer apart from the dominant hippie trend of the era. At Too Fast to Live, Too Young to Die, Vivienne Westwood sold custom-made zoot suits, alongside vintage denim, customised leather jackets and brothel creepers – a look that was deliberately designed to attract a different clientele from the Teddy Boys who'd frequented the King's Road shop when it was known as Let it Rock. Vivienne felt that the zoot suit was the foundation of rock 'n' roll style, a trend that came up from the streets, worn predominantly by Black Americans and Mexican immigrants, and thus a true symbol of counterculture. According to Vivienne, 'The surface of the Teddy Boy was full of racism, that's why we went through to the black roots that lay behind. We started to tailor really generously cut trousers, padded shoulders and double-breasted jackets, but we did it with feel. It was almost more than authentic.' In the 1940s, zoot suits had sparked a moral panic after a series of race riots spread throughout America, sparked by clashes between the zoot suit–wearing youth and those who took offence at the style and all it represented – prefiguring a similar moral panic that Vivienne and Malcolm would instigate with their pornographic T-shirts three decades later.

Smith Street Books

Published in 2024 by Smith Street Books
Naarm (Melbourne) | Australia
smithstreetbooks.com

ISBN: 978-1-9230-4909-3

Smith Street Books respectfully acknowledges the Wurundjeri People of the Kulin Nation, who are the Traditional Owners of the land on which we work, and we pay our respects to their Elders past and present.

Publisher: Paul McNally
Project editor: Aisling Coughlan
Editor: Emily Preece-Morrison
Design: Michelle Mackintosh
Illustrations: Helen Green
Proofreader: Pamela Dunne

Credits: direct quotes by Vivienne Westwood have been stated in various sources in the research of this book, including *Vivienne Westwood: Catwalk* by Alexander Fury, 2021; *Vivienne Westwood: an unfashionable life* by Jane Mulvagh, 1998; *Vivienne Westwood* by Claire Wilcox, 2004; *Vivienne Westwood* by Vivienne Westwood and Ian Kelly, 2015; *England's Dreaming* by Jon Savage, 2021; *National Geographic Fashion* by Cathy Newman, 2001.

Printed & bound in China by C&C Offset Printing Co., Ltd

Book 314
10 9 8 7 6 5 4 3 2 1

FSC
www.fsc.org

MIX
Paper | Supporting
responsible forestry
FSC® C008047